Original title:
Lunar Lunacy

Copyright © 2025 Creative Arts Management OÜ
All rights reserved.

Author: Lila Davenport
ISBN HARDBACK: 978-1-80567-873-1
ISBN PAPERBACK: 978-1-80567-994-3

Whimsy on the Cosmic Canvas

A sock in space floats with great grace,
It twirls around like it's in a race.
The stars wink down, the planets cheer,
As meteors zoom with a giggling sneer.

The moon wears sunglasses, what a sight!
As comets play tag in the shimmering night.
A rocket ship honks with a quirky tootle,
While space cows jump in zero-gravity hootles.

Aliens sip tea in a cosmic café,
While asteroids dance, they're here to stay.
One fell and slipped on a cosmic peel,
And laughed so hard, the void would squeal.

A nebula twirls in a colorful dress,
As planets gossip, what a lovely mess!
Gravity giggles at the cosmic jive,
In this funny dance, the universe thrives.

Reverberations of the Cosmic Dance

A toaster rockets through the starry expanse,
Crispy toasts bopping, they love to prance.
Galactic giggles bounce off each wall,
As the moon pulls a prank and starts to stall.

Stars play hopscotch on a comet's tail,
While a worm in a spacesuit tells a tall tale.
Jupiter's storms rumble like a DJ's beat,
As Saturn's rings spin in a swirling feat.

Dreamy space pigeons coo with delight,
Feathers float gently in the soft starlight.
Gravity's pull brings them closer still,
As they all laugh, it's a cosmic thrill.

An alien juggles with asteroids bold,
While space cats watch, their fur shining gold.
With a wink and a purr, they join in the spree,
In this zany universe, happy as can be.

The Twilight Gambit

In the glow of the night,
The raccoons take flight,
Stealing snacks from the porch,
Their giggles a torch.

The owls play chess,
With a wise, feathered mess,
Who knows who will win,
With a risky spin.

A squirrel dons shades,
In the moonlight parades,
While rabbits dance round,
To a whimsical sound.

Under the sly stars,
Fools drive tiny cars,
Letting laughter ignite,
In the soft, silver light.

Fantasies of the Moonlit Path

There's a dragon in bloom,
With a penchant for gloom,
He hiccups fireflies,
While munching on pies.

A frog in a tux,
Amidst whimsical ducks,
Sips tea through a straw,
It's the strangest of law.

The trees start to sway,
To the music of play,
While fairies in flight,
Juggle gnomes in the night.

Each critter's a star,
In their grasshopper car,
They race through the dew,
With a giggle or two.

Secrets Wrapped in Starlight

A cat with a hat,
Whispers secrets to bats,
About cheese from the moon,
And a dance with a tune.

Fireflies start to scheme,
In a whimsical dream,
Cooking up a delight,
For the party tonight.

The raccoons all cheer,
With a swing and a leer,
While squirrels plan a feast,\nWith apples at least.

In shadows they plot,
Each one a fine thought,
For the night's jovial tease,
Under cosmic trees.

A Cauldron of Cosmic Curiosities

In a cauldron, they brew,
With warts and a shoe,
A potion of giggles,
And spiced up wiggles.

Toads in capes perform,
With a jubilant charm,
While bats do a jig,
That's as big as a pig.

Stars bubble and pop,
As the moon takes a hop,
With ghouls pulling pranks,
In their ghostly hijinks.

What a scene they make,
With a chocolate cake,
Laughter fills the night,
In a zany delight.

Phases of Delightful Dissonance

When shadows dance on billowy sheets,
The moon winks its eye, oh what a feat!
Cats sing ballads with graceful flair,
As owls hoot, it's a grand night affair.

Beneath the glow, mischief takes flight,
Squirrels hold parties till dawn's first light.
With laughter and joy, the stars burst forth,
A cosmic giggle, from south to north.

Mysteries of the Nocturnal Sphere

The night wears a cloak of sparkling fun,
Where raccoons play tricks, just to stun.
Fireflies twinkle, a jolly parade,
As parked shadows seek their grand charade.

Beneath a sky of giggling beams,
The world swirls into silly dreams.
With wobbling chairs and dancing trees,
The moon grins wide, oh, such a tease!

Revelry of the Night Watcher

The starry host gathers with cheer,
Nightwatchers toast to ghosts drawing near.
With grinning gnomes and jolly sprites,
A raucous revelry of fun-filled nights.

Old myths unravel, like silly string,
As crickets dance and the cosmos sing.
Who knew the dark had such great style?
Mirth and mischief stretch for a mile!

Madness in the Moon's Embrace

Under a blanket of velvety blue,
Madness twirls in a jolly queue.
Bats wear hats, and foxes recite,
Silly sonnets that tickle the night.

The moon, a jester, throws pies with flair,
As laughter rings out, light as air.
In the folly of night, we twirl and we spin,
Where chaos reigns and the fun begins!

The Enigma of the Glowing Orb

Up in the sky, a big cheese wheel,
It wobbles and winks, an odd appeal.
Cats gather round, with eyebrows raised,
Plotting their heist, all night they gazed.

Dogs bark and howl at this cheesy sight,
While owls just stare, bewildered by night.
Bouncing stones seem to dance with glee,
As if they're chuckling, just wait and see!

Fragments of a Moonlit Dream

A rabbit in slippers hops down the street,
Wearing a hat made of fresh parsley wheat.
It giggles and flips, unbothered by clocks,
Whispering secrets to curious rocks.

The stars join in, sipping cosmic tea,
Debating if life's meant to be silly and free.
Floating candles dance on the breeze with flair,
In this midnight circus, nothing's quite fair!

Madness of the Night's Embrace

In a world where shadows begin to prance,
Squirrels wear boots and twirl in a dance.
The moon, quite flattered, throws confetti,
While raccoons audition, all cheers and confetti.

Frogs croak out tunes, with a jazzy beat,
While fireflies flash like they're stuck in a seat.
A ticklish breeze tickles all that it finds,
As laughter erupts and twinkles unwind.

Gleams of the Wondrous Globe

The globe above giggles, spinning with glee,
Lighting up mischief in every tree.
Pigs in pajamas roll down the hill,
While chickens play cards, all fluffed and still.

Bathed in its glow, the clowns feel at home,
Balancing spoons with a daring syndrome.
As night serenades, with chuckles and cheer,
Life's just absurd, let the laughter steer!

The Allure of Celestial Chaos

In the moonlight's gleaming rays,
Cats dance wildly, lost in plays.
Stars giggle with a twinkling wink,
While the universe spills its drink.

Socks vanish in the cosmic sweep,
As aliens twirl and jump with glee.
Planets spin in dizzy laughs,
Chasing comets, playing drafts.

Meteor showers rain down cheer,
Whispers of Mars tickle the ear.
A cosmic clown juggles bright,
Nutty antics all through the night.

Galaxies giggle in their chase,
Creating chaos in outer space.
Through the chaos, joy we'll find,
In this dance of the cosmic kind.

Pulses of a Starlit Heart

My heart beats to a starry tune,
With a rhythm that makes aliens swoon.
Sunbeams tiptoe, like a shy guest,
As I chuckle at this cosmic jest.

Space squirrels steal stars for their stash,
While meteorites race with a dash.
Jupiter's got a woolly hat,
And Saturn's rings dance; imagine that!

Asteroids skate on a moonlit slide,
While laughter echoes from inside.
Comets crack jokes, oh what a sight!
Robots fall over, what a delight!

With each playful twinkle above,
The universe beams with endless love.
So let's groove with a cosmic beat,
And dance with the stars, oh what a treat!

Night's Playful Reverie

In the dark, the mischief stirs,
A space raccoon sings and purrs.
Dreams ride comets, oh so swift,
As giggling planets play a gift.

A star drips laughter, glowing bright,
While shadows waltz in cozy light.
Winking moons play hide and seek,
Poking fun at the sleepy creek.

Night owls wear their glasses low,
Claiming wisdom from the flow.
With every quirk, the universe spins,
Tickling everyone, where joy begins.

So let's shout to the boundless skies,
As fireflies wink and tease our eyes.
In reverie, the stars declare,
The cosmos laughs, beyond compare!

Songs from the Silver Horizon

From the horizon, tunes arise,
Comets sing with joyful sighs.
Starfish strut in extraterrestrial shoes,
While galaxies throw a cosmic snooze.

A playful puff of cosmic breeze,
Twirling through like a cheeky tease.
Singing moons with a bobbing grace,
Turning night into a merry race.

Nebulas whirl with cotton candy,
Wishing one could join the dandy.
The Milky Way pours laughter's brew,
As space ducks waddle and coo.

Chasing light with each bonkers beat,
The universe bakes a sweet treat.
From the silver horizon, we'll aspire,
To dance among the stars, and never tire!

Surrendering to the Night

When shadows dance and giggles play,
The stars come out to party, hey!
An owl wears glasses, thinks it's hip,
While crickets clap, they just can't quit.

A cat in a hat starts to prance,
While fireflies join in the dance.
It's a raucous scene in the dark,
Even the moon joins in with a spark!

The trees tell tales with swaying laughs,
While shadows plot their silly crafts.
A raccoon steals snacks from a sleepy fox,
Beneath the glow of silver clocks.

So slip on shoes and come take flight,
Embrace the silliness of the night!
For laughter echoes with such delight,
In this whimsical realm, under starlit light.

Fantasies in the Fog

In the fog, where whispers tease,
A walrus croons with utmost ease.
He juggles fish, a slippery feat,
While seals applaud with flippers discrete.

The trees wear scarves, quite dapper and fine,
Murmuring secrets, just sipping on wine.
A fairy sneezes, and sparks fly bright,
Her wish just might turn wrong tonight!

A ghost with a broom will sweep the street,
Singing tango with two left feet.
Wandering through a curtain of grey,
They humor the fog in a comical way.

So wade through dreams, with joy and cheer,
Let giggles rise as you draw near.
In foggy fantasies, we shall feign,
The light-hearted tales that dance in the rain.

The Moon's Melancholic Muse

Old Luna sighs, a cosmic tease,
Painting sadness on gentle breeze.
But chuckles peek through her silver tears,
As crabs in tuxedos stage their cheers.

An old man moans while rocking his chair,
The stars just wink, they don't care!
With shadows in capes, they leap and glide,
While the moon just rolls, she cannot hide!

Her frown makes waves in the puddled dreams,
But laughter bubbles beneath her beams.
With every sigh, a chuckle flows,
In her lunacy, a humor grows.

So cozy up, let's share a laugh,
In moonlit tales, we'll craft a path.
For even in gloom, a spot of fun,
The night will dance until it's done.

Mythos of the Midnight Sun

At midnight's peak, the sun grinned wide,
Dressed in sunglasses with flair and pride!
A parade of owls hooted in style,
While rabbits marched, oh what a mile!

A penguin slid with a twist and twirl,
While foxes giggled, causing a whirl.
The sun just chuckled with rays of glee,
As stars clapped hands for the jubilee!

A dance-off broke out, wild and free,
With shadows shaking their memory.
Cactus grew legs just to join in,
A delightful dusk with a cheeky spin.

So let's toast pansies at this strange hour,
With giggles and joy, we'll feel the power.
For under the rule of the sun's bright fun,
The night brings more than simply undone!

The Folly of Moonstruck Hearts

Oh, how they dance beneath the glow,
Hearts aflutter, moving slow.
Chasing shadows, laughs collide,
Kissing the air where dreams reside.

Whispers float like balloons untied,
Giggling stars, a cosmic ride.
With every glance, the world's a stage,
Unruly love at every age.

Yet with each missed step they fall,
Tangled feet and silly sprawls.
A cheeky wink, a playful jest,
Turns the night into a quest.

In the end, as dawn draws near,
They'll swear they saw that waltzing deer.
With moonlit dreams, the truth we glean,
What folly is this, so utterly keen!

Echoes Beneath the Silver Veil

Echoes bounce through night's embrace,
As giggles shimmer, time's a race.
Underneath the veil so bright,
Fools merrily dance in the light.

Moonbeams whisper silly tunes,
To the antics of mischievous raccoons.
Chasing dreams with laughter loud,
A moonlit circus, merry crowd.

Every shadow plays a part,
A hilarity, a cosmic art.
Bouncing from the trees to ground,
In this madcap, joy is found.

When morning breaks with yawns and sighs,
They'll recall the fun with dreamy eyes.
Each echo lingers, sweet and spry,
With giggles still beneath the sky!

Skirts of Light and Folly

In skirts of light where jesters prance,
The moonlight joins their daring dance.
Who knew the night could be so bold?
With each twirl, laughter unfolds.

Mischief brews in silver streams,
Tickling souls, igniting dreams.
A comet's tail, a wink from fate,
Creating silliness we can't negate.

Skipping stones upon a lake,
They giggle loud with each big quake.
The stars above join in their scheme,
A cosmic party, a shared dream.

As dawn approaches with a sigh,
They'll wave goodnight beneath the sky.
For in their hearts, a spark alights,
From skirts of folly, oh, what sights!

Phantasmal Expanses of Night

Through phantasmal realms where shadows dart,
Playful creatures skitter, a work of art.
With giggles soft, they share the air,
A rendezvous beyond compare.

Each twinkle's a joke, each star a laugh,
In this cosmic game, they've found their path.
With silly wishes upon the breeze,
They chase the night, oh, such a tease!

The owls wink with knowing eyes,
As mischief brews beneath the skies.
In starlit whispers, tales unfold,
Of wacky dreams and secrets told.

With morning's light, the jesters flee,
But in their hearts, it's plain to see.
For in the dark, they soared so high,
In phantasmal nights, they learned to fly!

Twilight's Daring Dance

Under the moon's bright, silly glow,
Cats in tuxedos put on a show.
Frogs in top hats leap with flair,
While owls hoot tunes lost in air.

Stars twinkle, laughing all night long,
While fairies hum an off-key song.
Twirling fireflies join the spree,
In this dance of glee, wild and free.

From shadows leap the goofiest friends,
Spinning tales that never end.
A raccoon juggles with such grace,
As squirrels break into an acorn race.

With each step, the twilight sways,
In this zany, comic ballet.
So join the fête, don't be shy,
For the night wears giggles like a tie.

Cosmic Whirlwinds of Hysteria

In the galaxy where jesters prance,
Planets spin in a wobbly dance.
Shooting stars trip on cosmic beams,
While aliens plot their ice cream dreams.

Comets chase their tangled tails,
While moons serve up sparkling ales.
Asteroids play hopscotch near Mars,
As Saturn giggles, its rings full of scars.

Every planet has its quirks,
With Martians crafting playful smirks.
They hold a festival, what a sight!
Throwing confetti made of starlight.

Galactic frogs in silver shoes,
Leap to a tune, spreading the news.
In this space, the laughter's contagious,
As comedy reigns, oh so outrageous!

Eclipsed Revelations

The moon in shades of cheese and cream,
Casts shadows that tickle, or so it seems.
A rabbit winks in the night so dark,
While stars throw a humorous spark.

In the midst of a cosmic quirk,
Planets giggle, and comets lurk.
A sunbeam chases a mischievous sprite,
Who's stealing laughs, oh what a sight!

Jupiter's giggles echo far and wide,
As meteors take a joyride.
Whirling around, with gleeful spins,
While the universe chuckles, and the fun begins.

Behind the veil, the truth's a jest,
Unruly fun puts gravity to rest.
A dance of shadows leads to glee,
In this eclipse of jubilee.

The Celestial Jester's Game

High above where the fluffy clouds play,
A jester spins tales of night and day.
With juggling planets, and laughter so bright,
They prank the sun till it's out of sight.

The stars are a stage, the sky is a floor,
With each twinkle, they giggle and roar.
In cosmic capers, they engage in flair,
As comets crack jokes with wind in their hair.

"Hey, wanna race?" shouts cheeky old Mars,
While Venus rolls dice with the distant stars.
In this playful realm, mirth is supreme,
As laughter echoes like a sweet, silly dream.

So join the game, let your heart be light,
For the night's still young, oh what a delight!
In this folly of cosmic surprise,
Joy's the adventure that never dies.

Glimmers of the Unexpected

Beneath the moon, a cat does skate,
Chasing shadows that dance and prate.
A squirrel in shades, a tiny ballet,
All under silver light's display.

A frog in a tux, a party to throw,
Invites the stars, says, "Come, enjoy the show!"
They sip on stardust like a fizzy drink,
And giggle at tales of the sun's bright wink.

The owls wear glasses, a wise old crew,
Debating if cheese is truly blue.
As crickets tap dance, a shoe's a prop,
Laughter echoes till the night does stop.

A rabbit in socks conducts the fun,
Waving his arms till the rise of the sun.
With twinkling eyes, and a belly so round,
The night is alive with the silliest sound.

Portraits of Night's Ecstasy

A raccoon in a bow tie, quite dapper, indeed,
Steals a slice of cake, fulfills a sweet need.
He winks at the moon, so round and so bright,
And twirls in the dark, what a splendid sight!

Fireflies flicker, like starry confetti,
Making glow-in-the-dark pages all ready.
A dance-off begins, with flashlights galore,
As the critters compete on the woodland floor.

A hedgehog with style, with coconut curls,
Takes a bow on the stage, as the night twirls.
Chortles erupt, from a bush far away,
As laughter infections the world in dismay.

With marshmallows roasting, the warmth of the group,
Everyone joins in, a whimsical loop.
They trade their odd stories 'til bright morning light,
What a splendid spirit fills the magical night!

Moonlit Meditations of Delight

A turtle in shades, taking his time,
Contemplates life, with a slice of lime.
He dreams of surfing on waves made of cream,
Awaking shocked, but it's all just a dream.

A band of frogs, with guitars made of leaves,
Crooning their tunes, while the night softly weaves.
With splashes of laughter, a joke shared anew,
They sing about bugs that play peekaboo.

An owl with a monocle, wise and aloof,
Questions if squirrels prefer maple or goof.
He reads the night like a very best book,
While all the critters stop to take a look.

The fireflies sparkle, with rhythm and flair,
While a dancer's pirouetting without a care.
In this whimsical world where jesters take flight,
We find the wild joy hidden in the night.

Swaying to the Night's Melody

Bubbles in the air from a fizzy soda pop,
Tiny mice dance in a flip-flop hop.
With marshmallows bouncing and giggles galore,
The night is a canvas for laughter to score.

A porcupine juggles, quite the sight to see,
With woodland friends cheering, "You're wild and free!"
They toss acorns and berries with pride,
In a rhythm so silly, they can't help but glide.

Grasshoppers tap dance, with elegance rare,
While spiders spin webs that shimmer with flair.
Underneath stars that twinkle and play,
The spirits of laughter light up the way.

A possum in pajamas takes center stage,
Singing sweet ballads, uncaged by the age.
With each note they swoon, in the moon's gentle glow,
The magic of night makes the heart's laughter grow.

The Dance of Shadows

In the glow of night, they sway,
Silly silhouettes, leading the way.
With twirls and spins, they clap their hands,
Casting moonbeams on silver sands.

A cat with a hat joins the fun,
Dancing 'round like he's number one.
The stars giggle, the wind starts to tease,
As shadows tango with such great ease.

They prance on rooftops, laugh out loud,
Creating quite the raucous crowd.
Bouncing off walls, they skip and slide,
In a waltz where all can now abide.

As dawn approaches, they start to fade,
But promise of fun shall never jade.
So when night falls, come join the show,
For the dance of shadows will always flow.

Craters of Delirium

In a land where the cheese rocks roll,
Dancing mice delight in their goal.
Leaping craters, where giggles grow,
Silly wonders put on quite the show.

Aliens with hats made of cake,
Wobble and jiggle, for goodness' sake.
While cosmic cows moo in delight,
Sipping milkshakes under starlit night.

Hopscotch on craters, a joyful maze,
Counting the stars in a dizzy daze.
Winks from the sun, a cheeky tease,
As the moon launches into a sneeze.

Laughter bubbles like a warm cup,
As everyone gathers to shake it up.
In this madcap realm, here's the clue:
Funny faces are the moon's best view.

Tidal Temptations

The waves come in with a cheeky grin,
Pushing sandcastles, they want to win.
Drifting towels play hide and seek,
While flip-flops dance, oh what a peak!

Seagulls caw with a playful shout,
Stealing snacks, oh what a rout!
The tides tickle toes, a slippery race,
Making all giggle, what a funny place.

Mermaids wearing shades strike a pose,
Flipping fish-hair in the breezy flows.
Surfboards laugh as they ride the crest,
Each splash sends a grinning jest.

When the moon dips low with silver beams,
The ocean whispers its playful dreams.
So come this way, let laughter reign,
In tidal temptations, forget your chain.

Slices of Starlight

With cookies baked from cosmic dreams,
Starlight dances in sugary beams.
Baking joy in a galactic pan,
While sprinkles shoot like a shooting plan.

Comets glide on frosting trails,
Serving up laughter in starry scales.
Whimsical pies with a blueberry crest,
Delivering smiles with their sugary zest.

The universe giggles, a bright delight,
As it shares its secret recipes of light.
Planets swirl in a sugary waltz,
Cakes of laughter in celestial vaults.

When day breaks and starlight fades,
The joy lingers where the universe parades.
So gather 'round, enjoy the view,
For slices of starlight are meant for you.

Moonlit Madness

A rabbit hops in silver light,
Wearing shades, what a sight!
He dances by the old oak tree,
Shouting, "Look at me!"

The owls hoot a merry tune,
While cows jump over the moon,
A cat lassos stars with glee,
"Who knew it would be so free?"

The shadows play tag with the breeze,
Chasing giggles among the leaves,
A group of fireflies on parade,
Twinkling costumes they displayed.

In this chaos, all is bright,
Where each oddball finds delight,
With laughter echoing through the air,
In moonlit madness, we all dare!

Whispers of the Night Sky

Stars gossip with a twinkling grin,
Telling tales of where they've been,
While comets zip overhead,
Making wishes easier to spread.

A cheeky raccoon wears a crown,
On his head, he won't back down,
"I'm the ruler of this night!"
He proclaims as he takes flight.

Clouds waltz upon a breeze so light,
Frolicking in the soft moonlight,
While crickets play a symphony,
Of funny tunes, oh can't you see?

In this realm of playful dreams,
Where nothing is quite as it seems,
We join the whispers, laugh and play,
As night melts into a bright new day!

Celestial Caprice

A quirky star in polka dots,
Sips stardust tea from silver pots,
It spills and giggles with delight,
"Oh, what a silly, lovely night!"

Jupiter juggles moons so round,
While Saturn spins without a sound,
Galaxies laugh in cosmic waves,
Tickling comets, oh how they rave!

In a dance of sparks and gleam,
Each planet lives out a dream,
Shooting stars shoot silly jokes,
As laughter bursts from all the folks.

In this caprice, we find such joy,
As night plays tricks, our hearts employ,
With each twinkling wink from above,
We spin and frolic, wrapped in love!

Eclipsed Reflections

When the moon wears a shadowy cloak,
Silly whispers start to stoke,
"Hide and seek!" the stars all yell,
As giggles echo, who can tell?

A turtle sleeps on a crescent beam,
Dreaming big, living the dream,
While stardust drips from cosmic straws,
Creating silly giggles and applause.

Squirrels in stars play hopscotch fine,
While meteors zoom past in a line,
Each flash brings laughter, a quirky spark,
Lighting up dreams in the dark.

In reflections of this fun-filled night,
Where even shadows can feel light,
We join the cosmic dance, abide,
In eclipsed moments, laughing wide!

The Howling Lullaby

In the night, the wolves croon,
Dancing under the silver moon.
Hiccups echo in the trees,
As owls laugh and tease the breeze.

Cats prance in a furry parade,
Making shadows, unafraid.
Frogs wearing hats join the fun,
Jumping high, they start to run.

Beware the trolls with wobbly feet,
They trip and fall, can't take the heat.
While rabbits hop on pogo sticks,
Their silly antics are quite the mix.

So as the night starts to fade,
Wolves yawn, their howling waylaid.
Under this glowing, silly light,
Dreams are born in pure delight.

Beneath the Crescent's Spell

In the dark, a glow bemuses,
Little mice wear bright green shoes.
They dance beneath the crescent's beam,
Chasing stars, or so it seems.

A raccoon in a top hat grins,
Spinning tales of silly sins.
As shadows play hopscotch on the grass,
The possum offers sass, alas!

Crickets start a giggling choir,
Their tunes ignite the night like fire.
Fireflies flash in quirky ranks,
As jolly dreams sail on their pranks.

This gentle realm of whimsy swirls,
Where laughter twirls and mischief twirls.
So come and join this merry spree,
Beneath the moon, we all are free.

Radiance of the Restless Sky

Bubbles float on a midnight breeze,
Filled with giggles, check the cheese!
Stars like cameras click and snap,
As the night wears a merry cap.

Squirrels trade acorns for candy bars,
Shining brightly like little stars.
Clouds bounce, in a fluffy dance,
With every skip comes silly chance.

A hedgehog dons a cape so bright,
Wishing on a star tonight.
The moon smirks, it knows the game,
As laughter echoes, wild and tame.

Through this radiant, restless ride,
Critters revel, confidence wide.
Funny things in the night's embrace,
Every moment a silly chase.

Dreaming Under the Orb

Under the orb, a party blooms,
With gophers singing silly tunes.
Balloons float, tied to the trees,
As chipmunks dance, all with ease.

A llama struts in polka dots,
With clever jokes and tangled knots.
While the moon grins from on high,
Sending winks as time flies by.

Glowworms twinkle, leading the way,
To where the party is in full sway.
Wacky games and laughter loud,
Join the fun, be part of the crowd.

So jump in line, let's do the twist,
Under the orb, you can't resist.
Silly dreams take off in flight,
As we giggle into the night.

The Eerie Calm of the Unseen

In shadows where the night birds leer,
A cat wears glasses, oh so near.
The dogs plot mischief with a snicker,
As squirrels dance, their tails flicker.

A ghost of cheese floats by in jest,
With moonlit antics, they can't rest.
The owls in suits, they laugh so loud,
In their meetings, a wacky crowd.

The whispers twist, the owls conspire,
To start a band, their hearts on fire.
The trees applaud, their leaves a-clap,
While shadows giggle, a silly map.

As dawn creeps in, the fun takes flight,
The moon bids bye with a twinkly light.
In the day, the secrets packed,
Eerie calm, more mischief stacked.

Whims of the Wandering Star

A star skipped over, tripped on a beam,
And fell right into a cosmic dream.
With glittery shoes, it danced around,
Chasing comets without a sound.

It tickled Mars and winked at the sun,
Creating giggles in endless fun.
Gravity, who? It laughed in glee,
Spinning through galaxies, wild and free.

With planets joining in the chase,
They formed a line, a curious race.
The asteroids cheered, a raucous song,
As time raced forward, each twinkling throng.

When it finally paused to catch its breath,
The universe sighed, evading death.
Yet still it roams, with a cheeky spark,
Playing hide and seek in the dark.

Reflections on a Cosmic Tear

There once was a tear from a planet's eye,
A splash of laughter on the blue sky.
It rolled away, chased by the breeze,
Playing tag with the stars, if you please!

Each droplet giggled, a jolly tune,
As they leapt through the light of the moon.
They hit a nebula, made a big splash,
Creating rainbow waves in a cosmic crash.

A wise old comet, with a knowing grin,
Joined the chase, letting the fun begin.
They spun and twirled through the sparkling air,
To spread their joy, no one would care.

When morning came, the tear slipped away,
But laughter echoed, it's here to stay.
In the silence, the stars can't resist,
A chuckle lingers, a cosmic twist.

Bewitched by the Radiant Glow

Oh, the moon played tricks with a silver beam,
Casting shadows to stir up a dream.
The owls wore hats and sipped their tea,
While rabbits hopped in a wild spree.

Balloons floated through a giggling night,
As the stars twinkled with pure delight.
Each one a jest, a playful dare,
Winking at mortals, "Do you dare?"

A bumblebee buzzed, with a bowtie on,
Spreading cheer until the break of dawn.
It danced with daisies in crazy spins,
As crickets sang, wearing tiny fins.

Bewitched by light, the dreamers sway,
In this oddball tale, let's play all day.
With sparkle and giggles, we'll never slow,
In the whimsical realm of radiant glow.

Lunar Riddles in the Sky

Why did the moon wear a silly hat?
It thought it was a giant cat!
If stars could giggle in the dark,
They'd snicker at that shiny spark.

Aliens tease, 'What's with that face?'
Got caught in a cosmic race!
The craters laugh, they form a crew,
Making jokes that aren't quite true.

Comets zoom with a quirky rhyme,
Singing songs that stretch through time.
The night sky winks, plays hide and seek,
With grins that make the constellations squeak.

So stare up high, share a laugh,
Join the moon's quirky photograph.
For in the madness of night so wide,
The universe chuckles, full of pride.

Dances with the Nightlight

The moon put on its dancing shoes,
Bouncing around in a shimmering blues.
Stars twirled in a cosmic ballet,
Making wishes as they sway.

A rabbit jumped in a moonlit plot,
Hoping for carrots he'd never got.
He twirled and giggled with glee,
Shooting bright beams, wild and free.

When meteors fell, a confetti blast,
They laughed at moments that flew too fast.
The nightlight flickered, giving a wink,
As shadows played, adding to the brink.

So dance along with the starlit hype,
Embrace the night, it's all your type.
For in this waltz of whimsical cheer,
The laughter flows, we have no fear.

A Rhapsody of Radiant Whispers

In moonlit whispers, secrets prance,
The stars invite you to join their dance.
A meteorite off-key sings a tune,
Making mischief with a bright monsoon.

Oh, the sun's jealous, hiding away,
While the moons chuckle at the play.
A comet spins with a glimmering smile,
Tickling the night, oh, what a while!

Jupiter yells, "I'm the king of fun!"
But Saturn rolls on, adding more than one.
Galaxies swirl like a carnival ride,
As we giggle at what space can provide.

So take a seat in the starry dome,
This rhapsody of laughs feels just like home.
With radiant whispers that echo so wide,
Together we'll journey, side by side.

Staring into the Abyss of Night

Staring into the abyss so vast,
Wondering why the night flies past.
The darkness chuckles, holds its breath,
As shadows play at the edge of death.

Did you hear what the twilight said?
"It's just me, the night's not dead!"
The silence breaks with a silly boast,
Time to party with shadows, let's toast!

What's lurking in that starry sea?
A goofy ghost just grinned at me!
Echoing laughter from way up high,
Bouncing back from the midnight sky.

So dive into the giggles of night,
Join the laughter, it's outta sight!
In the abyss, with a twinkling glee,
Light-hearted dreams are wild and free!

Secrets in the Moonlight

A hamster in a tutu spins,
While cats wear shades, plotting sins.
The moonlight giggles, bright and sly,
And shadows dance, oh my, oh my!

An owl in jest, with glasses round,
Recites bad jokes in night's soft sound.
The trees all laugh at every pun,
As fireflies twinkle, having fun!

A raccoon juggles shiny spoons,
While crickets strum on crescent tunes.
The night is filled with laughter's roar,
As hidden secrets spill galore!

In this odd world, all seems quite right,
Reveling in the secret night.
For under stars, we lose all care,
In whimsical dreams, we float in air.

Constellations of Chaos

Up in the sky, the stars collide,
A penguin dances on a wild ride.
The comet's tail is made of cheese,
While squirrels plot to take the keys!

Mars is playing hide and seek,
While Pluto does a goofy sneak.
Jupiter lags in laughter's game,
Each planet adds to cosmic fame!

The Milky Way spills giggles bright,
As meteors race with pure delight.
Asteroids juggle, quite bizarre,
Creating chaos near and far!

In this vast sea of starry joy,
Every whim sparks like a toy.
As constellations wear silly hats,
The universe chuckles, oh how it chats!

The Insanity of Nightfall

A goat in pajamas leaps through the dark,
While bees play chess in a park.
The moon's a mischievous prankster too,
In a fedora, it winks at you!

The night spills secrets, giggles loud,
While owls cheer, forming a crowd.
A deer with candy canes prances by,
And butterflies sip from pie in the sky!

Raccoons debate about the best snacks,
As shadows plot against the cracks.
Underneath the swirling beams,
Reality's lost in playful dreams!

The sky swirls like a painted dream,
With laughter that sparkles and beams.
In this madness, all is fair,
As joy and folly fill the air!

Whimsy Among the Stars

A rabbit with a trumpet plays a tune,
While fish jump high to greet the moon.
Galaxies giggle, spinning bright,
In a quirky dance, all through the night.

Stars wear shoes that squeak and pop,
As planets tumble, never stop.
A jester comet, with a cheeky grin,
Tells tales of mischief, where to begin!

The sky is a canvas, wild and fun,
While lunatic laughter has just begun.
Each twinkle teases in glimmering glee,
In the grand game of cosmic spree!

Through strange worlds where whimsy lies,
With frolicsome creatures beneath the skies.
In the theater of night, we all play a part,
As the universe sings, a joyful heart.

Feasts of the Gathering Shadows

In the night, the shadows creep,
They gather round, a huddle deep.
With cakes and pies, oh what a sight,
The giggles rise under the night.

The owls bring salsa, the bats some cheese,
The moonlight glints, it's chilled with breeze.
While night critters dance, the fun ignites,
What a party in the starry heights!

The groundhogs serve and the raccoons toast,
Sipping dew like it's a fine roast.
They spin in circles, the stars they twirl,
A celebration that makes night unfurl.

So grab a slice of shadow's pie,
And raise a glass, you'll surely fly.
In this feast, where laughter's found,
The shadows feast, with joy abound.

Whirling Dervishes of Dusk

As twilight sends its dancing call,
The whirling dervishes start to sprawl.
They spin in robes of darkened hue,
Making merry in a winding view.

With each twirl, there's a hiccup learned,
A cackling laugh, for tables turned.
The stars above are swaying too,
They join the dance, in a cosmic crew.

The rabbits hop, in question mark leaps,
While crickets play, the melody creeps.
They ask the moon to waltz along,
And sing together their silly song.

With every whir, and every twist,
They conjure giggles that can't be missed.
As the night breathes in, and laughs with glee,
In twilight's arms, wild and free.

Dreams Adrift on Moonlit Waves

Floating dreams on silver seas,
With jellyfish giggles and bubbles of peas.
The waves, they chuckle, as stars do blink,
While wishing wells swim and boats get pink.

A catfish dons a tall top hat,
The octopus juggles, how 'bout that!
In this funny realm of dreams afloat,
Sea creatures dance, just like a boat.

The tide rolls in, with secret tales,
Of mermaids playing with nightingale trails.
They splash and play in moonlit hues,
While crabs do the cha-cha and sing the blues.

Oh dreams at sea, so odd and fine,
With giggly whispers in watery brine.
As the moonlight twinkles and waves collide,
In this frolic, we will all reside.

Fables of the Night's Keeper

The night keeper spins spun tales,
Tales of laughter on moonbeam trails.
With a flick of the wand and a wiggling grin,
Giggles erupt as the fables begin.

From silly knights and bickering trolls,
To dancing fireflies with luminous roles.
Each story a jigsaw, bright and bold,
A whimsical world, and laughter unfolds.

The moon it winks, with a knowing glance,
As shadows join in a merry dance.
Every creature laughs and plays their part,
With chirping crickets and peculiar art.

So gather 'round, with eyes open wide,
For the night's keeper spins from inside.
With fables of joy, no fear or dread,
Just funny stories until you're in bed.

The Delicate Thrill of Secrets

When the moon winks, the night gets wild,
Silly shadows dance, like a playful child.
Whispers float through the air, oh so sly,
Secrets shared with a giggle or a sigh.

Stars are blushing, having too much fun,
Ticklish tales under the glowing one.
The breeze, a jester, twirls and spins,
In this quirky world, where mischief begins.

Mischievous crickets play their tune,
While owls laugh at a satirical moon.
Every rustle, a chuckle in disguise,
Nature's comedy beneath the skies.

Who knew the night could be so absurd?
With giggles and gaffes, it's quite the word.
In shadows, the mysteries all collide,
A party of secrets, joyfully wide.

The Moon's Gentle Conspiracy

At midnight, the moon forms a cheerful plot,
Gathering starlight in a silver grot.
Dancing with clouds, a lover's tease,
Chasing away worries with charming ease.

The sun goes snoozing, while giggles rise,
The moon sends out beams for playful spies.
Squirrels gossip about the glowing face,
As laughter erupts in this secret space.

Mice tell tales of twilight's charm,
While shadows gather, raising alarms.
The moon's soft plot, a rave in disguise,
With nature's laughter under starry skies.

So if you peek into the night so bright,
You may just catch a glimpse of delight.
A gentle conspiracy, a comical show,
Where the moon and the stars steal the glow.

Tantalizing Tides of Night

The night rolls in with a cheeky grin,
Tides of laughter where dreams begin.
Glimmers of mischief from the sea so wide,
Pulling at hearts with the moon as a guide.

Crabs doing the cha-cha on sandy shores,
While the wave whispers jokes, oh the uproars!
Dolphins diving in, they join the spree,
In this tidal pool of whimsical glee.

Mermaids giggle, tails all a-flick,
Spinning wild tales with a magical trick.
The ocean sparkles with chuckles and cheer,
In these tantalizing tides, nothing to fear.

So come take a dip in this sea of delight,
Where laughter flows freely in the soft night light.
Dance with the waves, let your worries fly,
At the edge of the tide, under a canvas sky.

Dreamscapes in the Quiet Hours

In the quiet hours, where dreams take flight,
Whirling with joy, like a kite in the night.
Dare to wander where giggles abound,
In dreamscapes where whimsical thoughts are found.

Sugarplum creatures, in jammies they meet,
With marshmallow clouds where the laughter's sweet.
Dance in the twilight, so quirky and bright,
On pillows of fluff, while stars ignite.

Time tickles slowly, with each soft laugh,
As unicorns prance on a shimmering path.
A sprinkle of stardust, just for good cheer,
In this playful realm where joy appears.

So dream a little dream as the night unfolds,
With giggles and whispers, a story retold.
Embrace the absurd in the calm and the still,
In dreamscapes where laughter is the brightest thrill.

The Moon's Eccentric Embrace

In the night, she dances bright,
A waltz with stars, a silly sight.
Whispers tease on silvery beams,
Chasing shadows, giggling dreams.

Mice in tuxedos, owls wear hats,
As rabbits spin in polka dots.
She winks at clouds, a playful tease,
Painting the world with a cosmic cheese.

Balloons float by, on starlit breeze,
Tickling comets, oh what a tease!
Moonbeams slip on banana peels,
As laughter echoes, the cosmos squeals.

A caper of chaos, twirls and spree,
In her embrace, wild and free.
Join the fun, let worries cease,
In her glow, we find our peace.

Phases of the Unhinged

Bright and bold, she shows her face,
In a hat that's a little out of place.
With a grin that's wider than the sea,
She calls the night, "Come dance with me!"

Waxing, waning — what a show!
Jumpy shadows put on a glow.
Bouncing bunnies, singing ghouls,
Making party plans with silly rules.

Dressed in craters, spots galore,
She spins like a child — what's in store?
Giggles float on the twinkling air,
While meteors skate, unaware.

So grab your quirks, let's join the fun,
Share moon pie kisses, every one.
Through her phases, we laugh and play,
In the unhinged night, we'll sway.

Echoes of the Midnight Spell

Whispers ripple through the haze,
With a flick of her wand, she begins to amaze.
Cats in capes and frogs in shoes,
Stir the cauldron of midnight blues.

Brooms in races under her guise,
Each cackle sparks the starry skies.
A parade of oddities, join the quest,
Under her magic, we jest and jest!

Chasing fireflies, twirling about,
While tired gnomes snore, there's no doubt.
She chuckles softly, the night's glee,
A serenade of lunacy.

So cast aside the serious norms,
Join in the dance, twist through the storms.
For in the echoes, laughter melds,
With every spell, sanity yields.

A Celestial Serenade

She strums the strings of the night so bold,
With a laughter echoing, bright and cold.
Stars tap dance, join the band,
While planets sway, oh, isn't it grand?

Silly constellations hum and sway,
As shooting stars stomp all day.
Space critters giggle, gathering near,
Jellybean comets spreading cheer.

Moonlight beams bounce on the ground,
Their reflections flip, spinning round.
Waving hello to the sunlit dome,
The night sky feels just like home.

So sing with us in this cosmic spree,
Under the cloak of our melody.
Stars, they wink, with mischief and grace,
In this celestial, silly space.

Reflections in a Silvered Pool.

In the night, the frogs all croon,
With a croak that sounds like a tune.
They leap and splash without a care,
Dancing shadows float in the air.

Little fish join in the play,
Wiggling in their own ballet.
A moonbeam twirls, a gleaming prize,
While dragonflies wear party ties.

The silvered pool glints with delight,
As owls laugh in their flight.
A shimmering ball, a twilight feast,
Where giggles echo from the least.

All around the night is bright,
As critters throw a wild fright.
What a sight, what a show,
Underneath that twinkling glow.

Moonlight Madness

When the moon hangs like a cake,
You'll find squirrels wide awake.
Nuts are tossed like confetti,
While raccoons get all sweaty.

In the trees, the shadows dance,
As crickets leap in a trance.
With every hop, the grass does sway,
It's an odd, amusing ballet.

A fox wears a hat, quite bizarre,
While a cat strums on a guitar.
The night is a fabulous fair,
Full of quirks beyond compare.

The moonlight slips on banana peels,
Causing fits of laughter and squeals.
What a whimsical, wild spree,
Underneath that bright marquee.

Whispers of the Waxing Glow

In the garden, frogs feel grand,
Wearing hats made of soft sand.
Bees buzz about, throw a ball,
While flowers catch it, standing tall.

A mouse in slippers finds delight,
As the fireflies shine so bright.
Chasing after butterflies,
All in tune with the moonlit guise.

The whispers of the night surround,
With giggles floating all around.
What a silly, playful sight,
In the glow of that soft light.

So let's all join this merry dance,
And twirl around in a chance.
For when the sky begins to glow,
Even shadows want to show.

Celestial Illusions

Stars play tricks on the mind,
A sight that's one of a kind.
With a wink, they dance in place,
Creating mischief, just in case.

The moon, a giant disco ball,
Reflecting smiles, oh what a thrall!
Elves tap toes on rooftops tight,
Chasing dreams beneath the light.

A kitten rides a comet's tail,
While owls spin a curious tale.
What a jolly, funny scene,
In this cosmic, vivid dream.

So let the night not pass you by,
Find the joy, forget the sigh.
For in this whimsical escape,
Laughter wears the funniest cape.

The Mysterious Moonbeam

A beam sneaks in, oh what a sight,
It tickles toes in the dead of night.
Chasing shadows with glee and delight,
It dances on rooftops, full of mischief and light.

Old cats meow at the curious glow,
As squirrels debate if they should go.
The night feels silly, with giggles to show,
Even the stars are putting on a show.

The moon's a prankster, hiding in haze,
It gives the crickets their midnight praise.
While owls are hooting in playful ways,
The world laughs out loud in the moon's bright gaze.

What secrets it holds under playful beams,
Whispers of mischief, dancing in dreams.
The night is absurd, or so it seems,
With the moon as a jester, igniting our schemes.

Echoes in the Night

In the stillness, a laugh starts to creep,
A breeze brings tales, that tickle and leap.
Echoes of giggles, soft as a sheep,
Inviting all creatures from slumbering sleep.

The fireflies wink with witty delight,
While frogs form a chorus, singing all night.
The moon shares a joke, oh what a sight,
As shadows break out in a spontaneous flight.

A dog joins in, with a bark and a spin,
Even the trees start to sway in the din.
With laughter and whimsy, we feel the grin,
Of the night wrapping us in its silly skin.

Each echo a reminder, to dive into play,
To dance in the moonlight, to laugh while we may.
For the night's just a canvas, where dreams come to stay,
And every soft whisper encourages our way.

Secrets of the Midnight Realm

In midnight's grip, the secrets unveil,
Of critters who gossip, and giggle their tale.
They scatter and stammer, avoiding the pale,
Of moon's shining glare, like a ghost in a gale.

Raccoons wear masks, while owls raise their brows,
As fireflies scribble on cool darkened plows.
The shadows all shuffle, they giggle and wow,
At the sight of a cat chasing a flying cow.

The midnight realm spills with laughter so bright,
As whispers and chuckles dart left and right.
Even the rabbits decide to take flight,
Hopping and skittering into the night.

Lurking in corners, the chortles reside,
While moonbeams are sneaky, they giggle and bide.
In this realm, enjoy the whimsical ride,
For at midnight's peak, there's no place to hide!

Serenade of the Silver Sphere

Oh silver sphere, shining with glee,
You serenade shadows, hidden with spree.
Reflecting our laughter, wild and free,
As night plays a melody, a whimsical spree.

With giggles in harmony, stars join the play,
They twinkle and shimmer, so bright in their sway.
A tune for the dreamers, who wander astray,
While owls hoot a beat—come join in today!

Moonbeams are strumming on leaves as they hum,
While raccoons tap dance—oh look, here they come!
The night's a stage where all go quite dumb,
Chasing around, making noise like a drum.

So let the sphere serenade us tonight,
With laughter and joy, oh what a delight!
In this silly symphony, our hearts take flight,
As dreams swirl and twirl, in the glow of moonlight.

The Howling Silver Orb

The moon is round, it starts to grin,
And howling dogs, they join right in.
Cats in tuxedos dance in the park,
Making their rounds from dawn until dark.

Twirling shadows on the ground,
Skunks in bow ties, a sight profound.
Goblins giggle, their faces bright,
Under the glow of the shimmery light.

Squirrels with capes, they take to the trees,
Zipping and zooming with amiable ease.
Who knew the night brought out such flair?
Maybe a circus is lurking somewhere!

So raise a toast to the gleaming sphere,
For it brings us folly and wild volunteer.
With each twinkling star and wobbly jest,
We party and laugh while the moon does its best!

Nighttime Reveries

Beneath the twinkling glimmer and shine,
A cat on a skateboard dazzles in line.
He's pulling tricks, oh what a sight,
While owls cheer loudly, feeling just right.

Dancing fireflies play hide and seek,
It's an insect party, unique and sleek.
Crickets strum their tiny guitars,
As hedgehogs spin 'round under the stars.

Mice in pajamas waltz by the chair,
They drop their cheese, without a care.
The moon shines bright, casting dreamy beams,
While we chuckle loudly at our wildest dreams!

In this midnight carnival, joy's in abide,
As laughter echoes far and wide.
Tonight we celebrate under the moon's sweet tease,
When night turns fun, and all seem to please!

Fables Under the Full Moon

Once upon a time, under the glow,
A frog wore glasses, stealing the show.
With tales so wacky, he croaked with glee,
Of a snail who once raced a bumblebee.

A wise old owl, in a tweed blazer,
Scribbled stories about a quirky chaser.
Rabbits in bowler hats, sipping their tea,
Told yarns of adventures, wild and free.

While shooting stars played peekaboo,
The moon smiled down on this whimsical crew.
With jokes that twinkled and laughter that soared,
In silly fables, all spirits explored.

So gather around, let the tales unfold,
For under the moon, these stories are gold.
Every laugh shared in this enchanted night,
We dance in the joy as the stars shine bright!

Dreams Woven in Moonbeams

Under a canopy of shimmering light,
A parade of llamas prances in flight.
Dressed in piñata suits, what a sight,
They giggle and jiggle, what pure delight!

Alpacas whirl in a chummy ballet,
While fireflies flash their disco array.
Dreams woven softly of laughter and fun,
Playfully twirling until night is done.

The moon beams down, a cheeky muse,
As rabbits in tutus spread joyful views.
Socks on their paws, they leap with cheer,
Chasing shadows, their laughter we hear.

With dreams painted bright in this night of joy,
We revel together, no frown to annoy.
So let the moon shine on our merry parade,
And join in the fun, let's never evade!

A Cracked Cosmic Mirror

In the night I danced with glee,
My reflection laughed back at me.
The moon winked with a toothy grin,
"Look at the trouble you've gotten in!"

Stars giggled from their lofty perch,
As I tried to find a proper search.
Chasing shadows with flair and style,
My feet tripped over Saturn's dial.

Twirling cosmic dust in a haze,
I forgot which planet I should praise.
"Hey, Jupiter! You're quite a clown,"
As I stumbled, tumbling down!

With every bounce, my thoughts took flight,
Creating laughs that filled the night.
The universe chuckled in delight,
As I danced on in pure moonlight.

Errant Dreams and Starlit Schemes

Underneath a glittering sky,
I plotted ways to learn to fly.
With noodle arms and spaghetti legs,
I launched my mission, oh what a beg!

The stars conspired with mischievous beams,
Sending me wild, uncharted dreams.
"Catch a comet! Ride a moonbeam!"
I yelled while lost in a starlit theme.

Aliens snickered with chirpy sounds,
As I stumbled across zero bounds.
"Is that a flying fish?" they cried,
While I waved back on my cosmic glide.

In the end, I landed with style,
To countless giggles, and a cheeky smile.
The universe offered a cheeky cheer,
As I danced in dreams, free from fear.

The Light Between Lunations

There's a glow that winks at night,
A flicker of fun, a playful sight.
Between the moons that race and sway,
I find my joy, come what may!

I chased a shadow — what a mistake!
It jumped and giggled, "For heaven's sake!"
I spun around in dizzying airs,
With light that bounced, teasing my cares.

Planets chuckled in cosmic jest,
"Find your groove, this is a fest!"
I tried to pirouette in place,
But tripped on joy, a wild chase.

Beneath the glow of a cosmic grin,
I learned to laugh at the chaos within.
So here I dance, under starlit rays,
While the universe giggles, and endlessly plays.

Orbital Oddities

In a world that spins and twirls,
I wore my socks with polka-dots and swirls.
A telescope pointed at my clumsy feet,
Cosmic laughter echoed on every street.

Saturn rolled its ring with flair,
"As you stumble, do you dare?"
I waved back, in a daze,
"Is this the best of all cosmic plays?"

The sun chuckled, "You're quite the sight!"
As I danced awkwardly in the light.
Planets spun like tops on high,
As I flipped and flopped, oh my, oh my!

Every mishap became a cheer,
As laughter filled the atmosphere.
With every twirl and every spin,
The carnival of stars danced in.

Celestial Cirque of Shadows

In a circus of twinkling stars,
The moon juggles comets and Mars.
Laughing craters do backflips in glee,
While shadows play tag behind a tree.

A ringmaster made of stardust and dreams,
Directs the show with whimsical beams.
Ghostly acrobats dance in the light,
As we giggle at the charming sight.

Bright halos of laughter float in the air,
The sun joins in, just to be fair.
The clowns are made of moonbeams and dust,
In this cosmic show, we absolutely trust.

Underneath it all, a silly surprise,
You'll find bright chuckles in starry skies.
So let's take a seat and enjoy the fun,
At the celestial show, we're all the ones!

Laughter in the Ethereal Light

In a glow where giggles take flight,
The stars play tag in the soft twilight.
Moonbeams shimmer with cheeky delight,
Can you hear the laughter? What a sight!

Whispers of joy drift on the breeze,
As crickets croak out their silly tease.
Fireflies twinkle with fairy flair,
Doing the cha-cha while floating in air.

A cat in a bowtie struts down the lane,
Chasing his tail, oh what a game!
Silly shadows prance just for fun,
Under the gaze of the watchful sun.

So gather around, let's share a cheer,
In this ethereal glow, there's nothing to fear.
With laughter as bright as the glowing night,
We'll dance like our dreams take flight!

Haunting Echoes of the Night

The owls hoot jokes from their spooky lair,
As bats flap by in a hilarious scare.
Ghosts with their sheets do the waltz,
Causing slight tremors and laughter's false faults.

With echoes that bounce through trees so high,
The night is alive with a ticklish sigh.
Skulls tap-dance on graves with such flair,
While the moon chuckles at their wild affair.

Whispers of pranks float on the air,
A friendly ghost pulls chairs from thin air.
The shadows plot with mischievous delight,
Ready to share in this ghostly night.

So let's join the parade of haunty glee,
In this realm of whimsy, we're all set free.
With laughter infused in the cool night so bright,
We revel together, oh what a sight!

The Enchanted Glow of Dusk

As the day gives way to playful night,
Colors swirl in the fading light.
The sun bows down with a gentle cheer,
Inviting giggles from far and near.

With fairies tossing sparkles so round,
The air is filled with a laughter sound.
Crickets break into a tap-tap tune,
While stars play peek-a-boo with the moon.

The breeze carries secrets and little sighs,
From the animals with their twinkling eyes.
A raccoon wearing a tiny hat,
Winks at the world like, "Imagine that!"

Gather 'round as dusk takes its call,
In this enchanted glow, there's room for all.
With chuckles and grins, let our joy abound,
In the cozy embrace where laughter is found!

The Moon's Mischievous Grin

In the sky she winks at me,
With a light that bends so free.
Humans dance, with silly glee,
As she pulls the tides, oh see!

Clouds hide her, a peek-a-boo,
While owls hoot their wise adieu.
Balloons float, as dreams ensue,
All because she found her crew!

Neighbors yell, 'What's up tonight?'
As shadows prance in pure delight.
Chickens cluck with all their might,
Suspecting something's not quite right!

So let's celebrate her grin,
With capers bold, and playful spin.
For under her beam, we begin,
To dance like fools, let's dive right in!

Chasing Shadows at Twilight

The sun dips low, the day's undone,
Now creatures creep, it's just begun.
With giggles loud, and silly fun,
We chase our shadows, everyone!

Sneaky cats, they stalk and pounce,
While we pretend to leap and bounce.
The moon, she chuckles, like a louse,
As we get lost in gold's renounce.

Silly ghosts, they play their game,
Scaring us, but it's all the same.
In the twilight, we stake our claim,
And jump around, without a shame!

Echoes of laughter fill the air,
With silly hats and wild hair.
In this twilight without a care,
We chase the night with joyful flair!

A Symphony of Starlit Whimsy

A twinkling band plays out there,
With starry notes to fill the air.
Comets zoom while we all stare,
A whimsical show beyond compare.

Jellybeans rain from a bright sky,
As candy clouds drift lazily by.
We dance beneath, our spirits high,
Singing silly songs, oh my, oh my!

Planets bop in a cosmic huddle,
While moonbeams shake in merry puddle.
Jokes on Mars—"Hey, don't you muddle!"
As Saturn jingles, laughs on a cuddle.

What a night for fun and jest,
With galactic friends, we're truly blessed.
In the starlight, we take a rest,
And dream of sweets, oh what a quest!

Spellbound by the Night

Nighttime casts a silly spell,
With laughter ringing like a bell.
The moon is here to weave and dwell,
In a world where whimsy swells.

A raccoon steals snacks from the ground,
While fireflies dance, a glowing round.
Silly hats are all around,
In a night of fun, where joy is found!

Dancing in pajamas, wild and free,
We twirl and giggle like a jubilee.
The spell of night, a libretto glee,
As stars join in, a cosmic spree.

With jokes and tricks that make us grin,
Carried on breezes, we spin and spin.
When morning comes, we'll paint again,
This night of laughter, where it all begins!

www.ingramcontent.com/pod-product-compliance
Lightning Source LLC
Chambersburg PA
CBHW051638160426
43209CB00004B/699